This book belongs to:

....

Inside your *Knights, Dragons and Castles Sticker Activity Book*, there are lots of fun things for you to do! Use felt-tip pens to doodle and colour, but don't forget to leave them to dry to make sure they don't smudge. You'll find all the stickers you need to finish the pictures in the middle of the book.

Have fun!

Scholastic Children's Books,
Euston House, 24 Eversholt Street,
London NW1 1DB, UK

A division of Scholastic Ltd
London ~ New York ~ Toronto ~ Sydney ~ Auckland
Mexico City ~ New Delhi ~ Hong Kong

Edited by Catharine Robertson

Published in the UK by Scholastic Ltd, 2014

Illustrated by Tom Knight
© Scholastic Children's Books, 2014

ISBN 978 1 407 14787 1

Printed in Malaysia.

2 4 6 8 10 9 7 5 3 1

All rights reserved. Moral rights asserted.
This book is sold subject to the condition that it shall not, by way of trade or otherwise be lent, resold, hired out, or otherwise circulated without the publisher's prior consent in any form or binding other than that in which it is published and without a similar condition, including this condition, being imposed upon the subsequent purchaser.

Papers used by Scholastic Children's Books are made from woods grown
in sustainable forests.

Welcome!

Welcome to Godfrey Castle! This is the home of Lord Godfrey and his family. There are also lots of knights who live here. They defend the castle against fierce dragons. Use the stickers in the middle of the book to complete the castle scene.

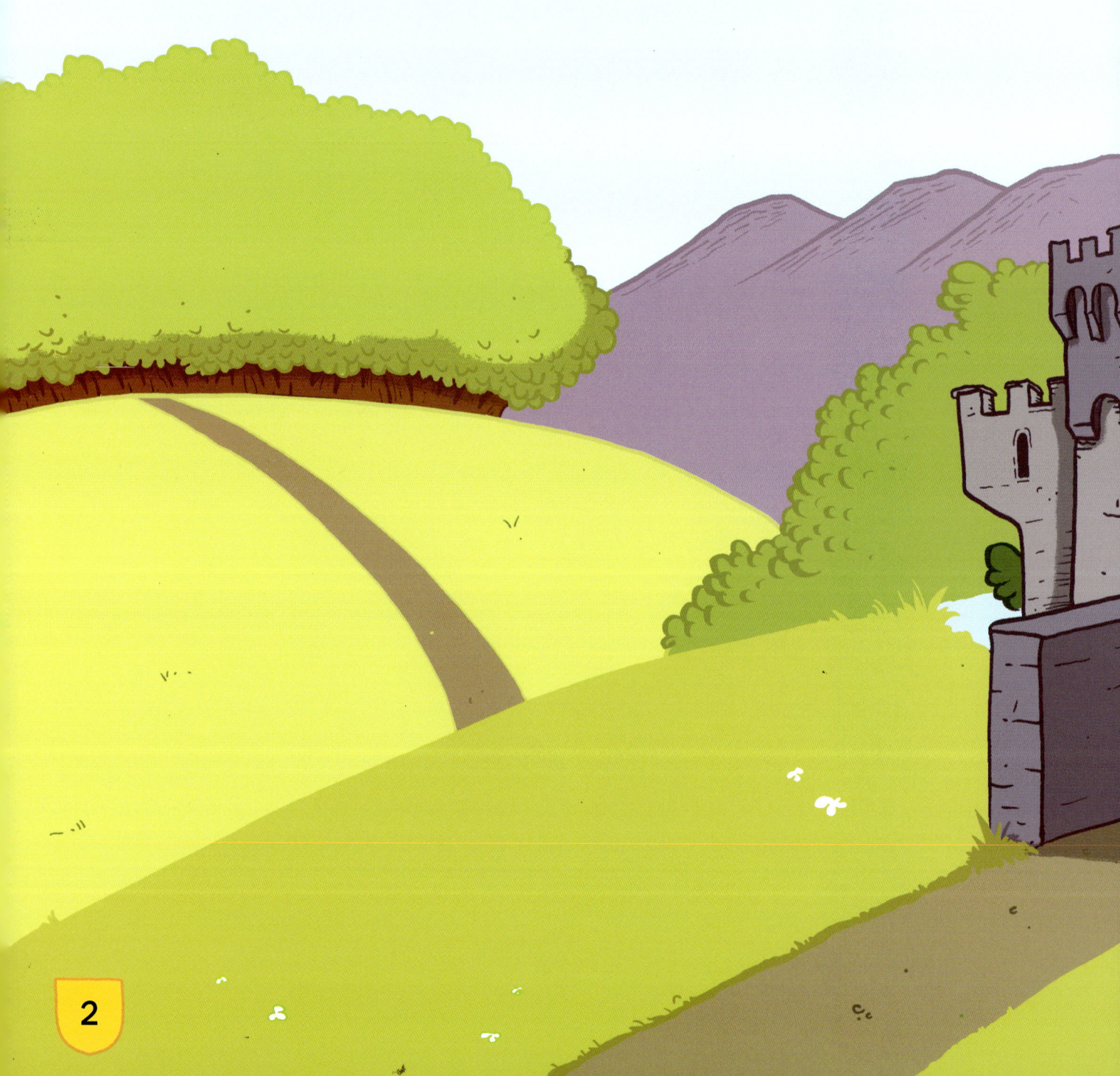

In Training

These young squires are learning how to become knights. They have to learn lots of different skills. Use your stickers to finish the scene.

Coat of Arms

When the knights wear armour, they all look the same. So each knight has a picture on his shield to tell them apart. Use felt-tip pens and stickers to design a shield for yourself on the next page.

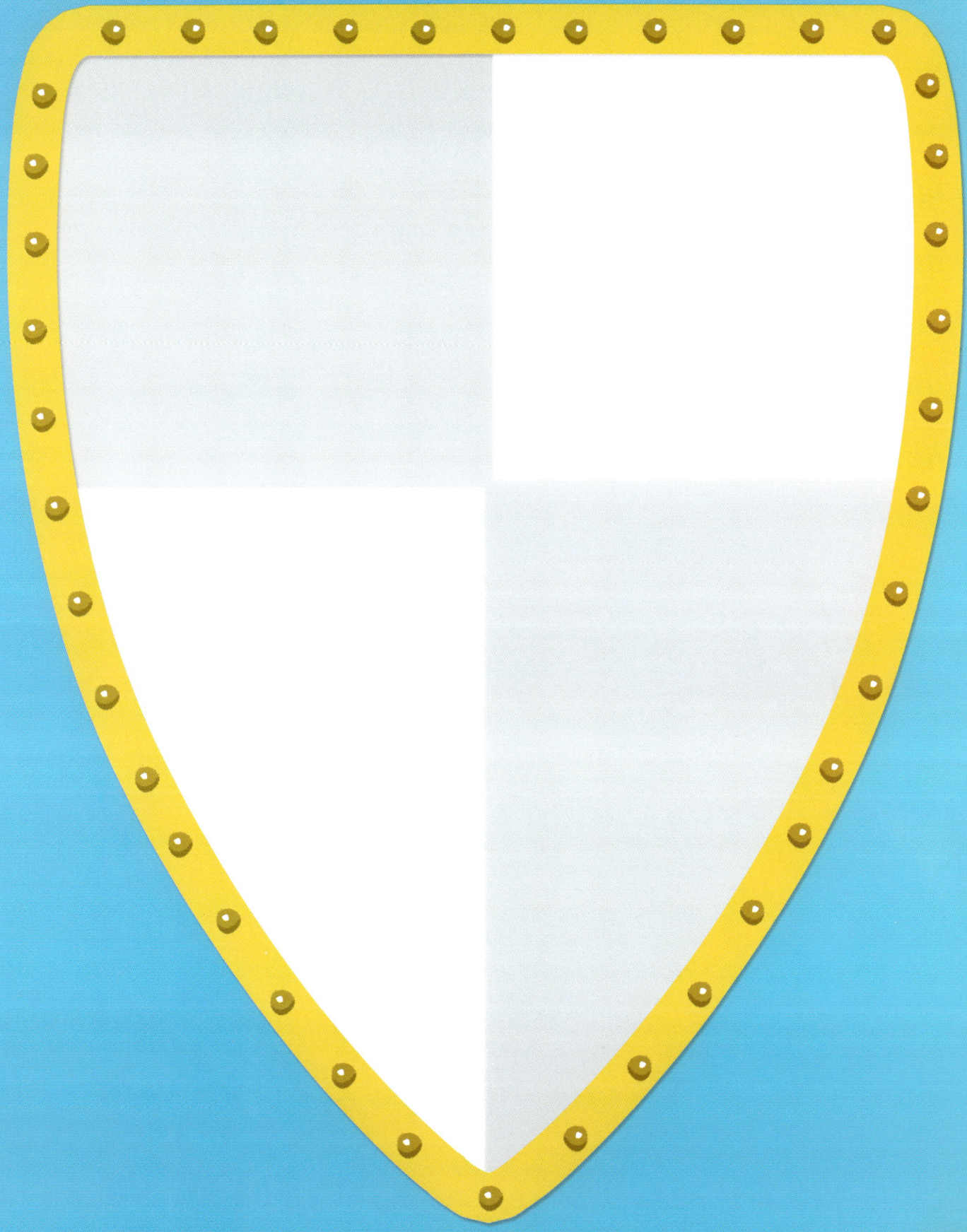

In the Courtyard

It's not just knights who live in the castle – there are lots of other people too. Can you spot 5 children, 4 ladies, 3 dogs, 2 guards and 1 jester?

Horses

Each knight has his own horse. So you know whose horse is whose, the horses wear colourful outfits to match their knight's coat of arms. Use felt-tip pens and stickers to decorate this horse so he matches his knight.

Can you work out which horse belongs to which knight?

Dragons!

Lots of dragons live deep in the forest behind the castle. These mummy dragons are trying to protect their eggs from the knights, so they've hidden them. How many hidden dragon eggs can you spot? Use the stickers to mark each egg when you find it.

Egg-cellent

Dragon eggs are very beautiful. Use felt-tip pens to make them as colourful as you can and stickers to add cool patterns.

Which Knight?

The knight you're looking for is riding a black horse, he has a blue shield with a lion on it and he's not carrying a lance. Can you circle the right one?

Welcome! (pages 2 and 3)

In Training (pages 4 and 5)

Coat of Arms (page 7)

In Training Continued

Horses (page 10)

Dragons! (pages 12 and 13)

Egg-cellent (pages 14 and 15)

Tournament (pages 18 and 19)

Up, Up and Away! (pages 20 and 21)

Hidden Treasure (pages 24 and 25)

Celebrate! (pages 30 and 31)

Dot-to-Dot

Join the dots to see who is flying over the forest.

Tournament

Godfrey Castle is hosting a big tournament. This is a special competition where knights show off their skills and bravery. Use your stickers to fill the field with competing knights and lots of excited people.

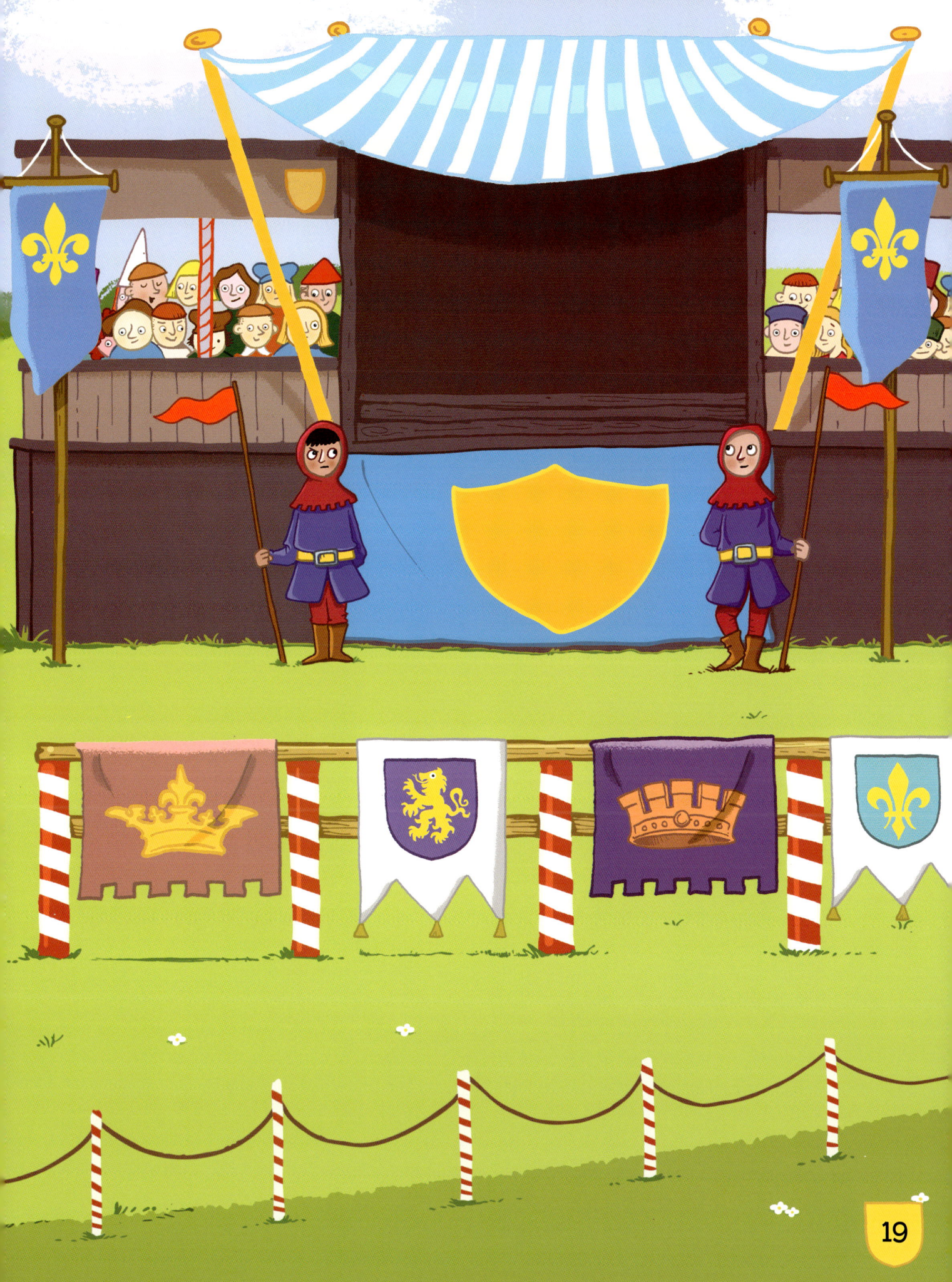

Up, Up and Away!

The dragon babies have hatched and they're learning to fly.
Use your stickers to fill the sky with dragon babies.

What's Changed?

The tournament has begun! The first competition is the jousting. Can you spot eight differences between these two pictures of jousting knights?

22

Hidden Treasure

Oh no! While everyone was at the tournament, the dragons stole some treasure from Godfrey Castle! They have hidden it in a cave deep in the forest. Use your stickers to add more sparkling treasure.

Knights in a Tangle

The knights are out riding in the forest trying to find the stolen treasure. Which knight is going to reach the cave where the treasure is stored?

Riddle

Sir Henry has found the cave, but now he must solve a riddle to get past the fierce dragon and rescue the treasure. Each letter of the message has jumped back one place in the alphabet. Can you help him crack the code?

h vhkk ezkk zrkddo he xnt rhmf z rnmf

Mighty Maze

These knights are on their way back to the castle with the treasure, but first they must get through a mighty maze. Can you help them find their way home? Don't forget to colour in the castle too.

Celebrate!

The knights are home at last, so Lord Godfrey is hosting a big feast in their honour. Use your stickers to fill the scene with delicious food, musicians and the castle pets.

All the Answers

Pages 8-9 In the Courtyard

Page 11 Horses

Horse A belongs to Knight 3
Horse B belongs to Knight 4
Horse C belongs to Knight 1
Horse D belongs to Knight 2

Pages 12-13 Dragons!

Page 16 Which Knight?

Page 17 Dot-to-Dot

It's a dragon!

Pages 22-23 What's Changed?

Page 26 Knights in a Tangle

Knight 2 made it to the treasure cave! Did you get it right?

Page 27 Riddle

I will fall asleep if you sing a song.

Pages 28-29 Mighty Maze